BESSIE'S RESURRECTION

ALSO BY KIMBERLY A. COLLINS

Choose You! Wednesday Wisdom to Wake Your Soul

Slightly off Center

BESSIE'S RESURRECTION

Poems

Kimberly A. Collins

INDOLENT BOOKS

Cover art: Sam Grisham
book design: adam b. bohannon
Book editor: Samantha Pious

Published by Indolent Books,
an imprint of Indolent Arts Foundation, Inc.

www.indolentbooks.com
Brooklyn, New York
ISBN: 978-1-945023-21-7

Special thanks to **EPIC SPONSOR** Megan Chinburg for helping
to fund the production of this book.

CONTENTS

SONG OF FLIGHT

SONG OF FATE

AUTHOR'S NOTE

In Richard Wright's *Native Son* (1940), it is Bessie Mears who supplies the soundtrack for Bigger's story. Bessie's articulation of her experience as an African American woman and how she suffers in her unenviable position, powerless and unseen, is delivered within Wright's text as a spoken-word blues ballad rather than a Bessie Smith blues song. Bessie's plight provides entry not only into her life but also into the real lives of African American women.

Here, Bessie's fictionalized character is self-actualized together with two trailblazer African American women: Bessie Smith and Bessie Coleman, who lived during the same time period and who share her name. These poems, which re-imagine their lives, are a microcosm of the lived experiences of African American women who face violence, limitations, and challenges. Their voices and bodies are resurrected to articulate their ideas of worth, to claim a space to speak not only for themselves but also for their sisters who have been left voiceless. Their lives become three songs which are analogous to the three parts of *Native Son*: Fear, Flight, and Fate. While it is Bessie Smith who supplies the soundtrack to *Bessie's Resurrection*, this collection, written for all three Bessies, honors Black women as the necessary backbone to the fight against being buried alive.

This book is dedicated to my Sister Wendy
and my Spelman Sister Tiffany Austin.

You are gone and not forgotten.

So de white man throw down de load and tell de nigger man tuh pick it up. He pick it up. He pick it up because he have to, but he don't tote it. He hand it to his womenfolks. De nigger woman is de mule uh de world so fur as Ah can see.

                ❧ Zora Neale Hurston, *Their Eyes Were Watching God*

Words or thoughts shared, but not acknowledged, are like
Birds of wisdom flying towards their destination—but never arrive.
Patches of material saved for a magnificent quilt which remain
    unassembled.
A gift given out of love; filled with secrets, surprises, laughter, joy,
    anger, and pain
Yet never opened. Those revelations are lost.

                            ❧ Georgia Hopkins

PRELUDE

Bessie's Gospel

"Sisters and Bruthas we met heah on some serious bizness. It's been some back–bitin' going on and the thing I wants to know is who's been doin' it? It's a shame! It's a shame! It's a shame! The thing I wants to know is what bit me on mine? I mean, who bit me on my back?"

VERSE 1
Our blues breaking a black belt of sky   disappearing
shards of yellow saved by sunrise   stubborn to be gone.
Souls howling our blues of misery   voices strumming one sound

CHORUS
You better get down on your knees
and let the good lord hear your pleas
cause if you want to rest with ease

Moan. You moaners

VERSE 2
A place where mahogany women grow
find whole pieces of themselves in green shrubs and magnolia trees.
A winding street, where brandy-colored men scatter
where sistahs lean ovah window sills under a yam-colored sun
elbows touching one stone.

Just bend your head way down and pray
to have the devil chased away
come let your souls be saved today

Moan. You moaners

VERSE 3

Even my death wasn't easy. An untethered thing drifting, tumbling
spying abandoned bodies. Daughter of mine. Born of my blues.
Born to risk flight. Stuck in fright. Bessie's blues. My wings.
The spit that makes me fly past Union Stockyard. A penned fate.
I have no sympathy for the caged birds that only sing. I am born again.

CHORUS

You better get down on your knees
and let the good lord hear your pleas
cause if you want ta rest with ease

Moan. You moaners

VERSE 4

Even my death was not easy. But there. Beyond Philly.
Beyond Chicago. But there, beyond Jim Crow's
love for me. Wails ruffle bearded sycamore trees.
Dust covers my landless feet that busk, stomp my blues.
A wooden floor band possesses me. In daddy's church.
Standing in sanctified tones saved for 13th and Elm St.

CHORUS

Just bend your head way down and pray
to have the devil chased away
come let your souls be saved today

Moan. You moaners

Whole family. Every Sunday. After church. Grandma's face a fist. I
  remember.

On my knees. Askin' God to hab mercy. On me. Abandoned.
  Silenced. I'm told.

Her blues be wicked. Bessie is not holy. Bessie's blues are my glory
  clothes. I am

the residue of her blues. She tastes me across time. Bessie cradles my
  blues.

Rocks in me a new religion. Almost as good as whisky.

CHORUS

You betta get down on your knees
and let the good lord hear your pleas
cuz if you wanna ta rest with ease

Moan. You moaners

Just bend your head way down and pray
to have the devil chased away
come let your souls be saved today

Moan. You moaners

SONG OF FEAR

Elisheba

An oath pledged to God.
She blinks as a nectarine sun slices dawn
leaning into shade against a baobab tree.
She's a tiny thing. Her breasts have not begun to bud;
onyx eyes sparkle as giraffes give awkward glide
zebras prance in praise. She is safe/   Winds shift.
Blades of grass wriggle between her toes.
She doesn't notice the animals halt/   away from the open plain.
Too late. Her feet bolted. Hands tied to splintered bark.
She struggles. Dankness robs her day/   Feces/
urine/ supplant smells of her mother's
peanut stew
left burning on an open flame.
She is Elisheba, a scattered prayer.

Bessie's Lost Song

My name nestled navel deep
Sheba shushes me in her breast
Elizabeth bawls a half-sound
Liza
Beth
Bess
sing arias for me
Elisheba   our namesake   with tear-stuck lashes
I'm part of her lost song

3 Bessie Bop

If I should fly this way again, I'd still
plow cotton-field skies—fearless.
Chocolate-dipped wings will hover
break   free. Currents twist. Him
bucking wind. Flying with me
this time. I scrape ground.

I've gotta sad sad story today
I've gotta sad sad story today
I'm goin' to the gin house when the whistle blows

I'll learn the hail Mary and the praise dance too,
throw myself over Jesus' bent knee, curtsey past
this life of misery: *All my life's been full of hard*
trouble. If I wasn't hungry I was sick. If I wasn't sick
I was in trouble. I ain't never bothered nobody. I just
worked hard every day. I had to get drunk to forget it.
I had to get drunk to sleep. I wish to God I never seen
Bigger. I wish to God *one of us died before we was born.*

I've gotta sad sad story today
I've gotta sad sad story today
I'm goin' to the gin house when the whistle blows

We weren't apron-dressed women.
Nothin' natural was gonna kill us. It had to be
something stronger than wind, brick or car.
All my life spent singin' blue notes to be seen.
Singin' somethin' about being black and being woman.
Being black and blue, being black and beautiful too.

I've gotta sad sad story today
I've gotta sad sad story today

I'm goin' to the gin house when the whistle blows
My troubles come like rain that's all been poured before

EEE you sinners, hear my call
Satan's waiting for you all
Better get your souls washed white
Better see the light ... AMEN
Bessie Smith, "Moan, You Moaners"

A Long Blues Note

And it's a small church on the Negro side of town where they gather, shoulder strong as one voice in their Glory to God. Praising him for the trouble they've seen, and the low valleys made high. There is no casket for this woman named Bessie. The Coroner took her for bodily evidence. It is a misery memorial for a brown girl dead. It could have been any of these cinnamon-, cumin-colored souls. Somebody needs to cry for her. Their sagging shoulders slumber against one another until one of the Church mothers breaks ranks with the somber sleepers to raise her floral hanky and asks the Preacher: "Why Bessie?!"

a burning lesson

Iron teeth kiss   her ear lobe, hiss
down her spine. She misses discarded pink
ribbons wound tight around plaited braids.

Some girlfriend said it was time.
Mary Janes and white ankle socks
be handed down, cotton hair bows too.

Cupping her ear, Bessie sat almost still—spying
steel comb's spilling heat, promising straight
edges, gaining momentum to correct her beauty.

A slight movement in the wrong direction.
The first scorch of being grown.

Washer Woman

Wrinkled fingers wring excess.
Clothes pinned lips, she hangs the bright

with the faded. The same weight—
time makes them blend.

Seeing his dreams flapping, drip-dried
in Chicago's soot-sprinkled wind,

daddy removes his load.

My mother's weather-worn hands
pass me pins. I hang mixed colors

we wear in prayer for a forgiving wind
to not

blow away labor we have learned to trust.

Just hear those sisters groanin',
And hear those brothers moanin',
Repentin' and atonin'...
—Bessie Smith, "On Revival Day"

UPSOUTH

I never wanted to go to Mississippi
Momma's momma still there yearnin' for visitin' kin
She say folks don' starve like dey do up here
Mississippi's magnolia trees never held no charm for me
only hypnotizing loose ropes swingin' in front of me
Can't convince me Mississippi better than Chicago
New York, Philly or any northern city even if they
lynch with iron ropes and bonfire chairs.

Bessie's Cry

My wails bounce off cramped scratched
walls.
More spent on gin than rent.
Drinking up men.
Tipping bar stools with time.
No way out of this life alive.
Snaggletooth women look at me as memory.
These women are not always wise.
My momma was one; sat me on laps for a dime.
Before I was ten, my hips ached with the rhythm of men.
Played giddy-up-horsey without a nursery rhyme.
Clicking tongues knitted my skin.
A fitted sweater without holes for escape.
My mouth, parched with desire. A desire I'm not sure is mine.
Wanting and wanted, hunting and hunted   all the same to me.
My head hurts.   Crushed between fist   and sky.

I never loved like that, loved like that since the day I was born
I said for fun, I don't want you no more.
—Bessie Smith, "Outside of That"

Waiting on Bigger

Leaning slack against my pale green
grease-stained wall, I smell my sweat—

cold. Round, wet, polka dots plastered
on my cotton dress, caved between

damp legs. My lips. Venus grapes,
pucker, pout together, like my thighs,

wishing to shout. Waiting
for his knock and to be bent

over the cool side of my stove.

SHE Song

A woman can love a man more than she
A woman can love a man more than she
O yes she can

A woman can love a man
A woman can love a man
O yes she can

She can give her money
She can give her soul
Give all of her with no return

A woman can love a man more than she
A woman can love a man more than she
O yes she can

She give her time
She give her dime
She don't give a damn
she lovin' that man more than she

she give her whole self   whole
she give her whole self   whole

A woman can love a man like that
A woman can love a man like that
O yes she can

Kicked in the gut
with love's steel toe
Kicked in the gut
by love's steel toe

Lovin' that man the way she do
Lovin' that man the way she do
She sorrow got no place to go

Have you ever seen a church begin to rock?
Heard a sundown deacon preachin' to his flock?
Have you ever seen old Satan on the run?
Then follow me, see just how it's done
—Bessie Smith, "On Revival Day"

Bessie's Good Day

Damn!
Bessie must've had at least
one good day
a day when she was waiting
on grand-mom's biscuits   hot
licking butter   streaming   down her mouth
A day when she and some
butterscotch   vanilla wafer
chocolate chip   peanut butter
flavored   delicious women
shared   deep belly   laughter
their fingers turning soil—straightening each other's crowns
with Dixie peach love
snapping beans in rhythm
to home-spun gossip
or twisting their bodies   on bar stools
moving their butts   to blues tunes
A day when Chicago's breeze   is held back by an impatient sun
beaming down on her brown shoulders
her hips pointed   east and west
her naked legs tickled by the hem of a bright-colored sundress
giving a sway to her walk
black men straddling
street corners   whistling their appreciation

A day when Sunday joy knocks her pillbox hat askew
bursts gold-plated buttons on her red
dress exposing ripe breast
Old saints' heads   graced with lace
their white cotton gloves wiping   tears of deliverance
from her face
while Sunday morning soles
tap dance   praise
stomp out *Amen*

not the lindy hop or the other dances she knew
some good days when whisky breath smiles   broke free

Gee, but it's hard to love someone
When that someone don't love you
I'm so disgusted, heartbroken, too
—Bessie Smith, "Down Hearted Blues"

Bigger's Brick

After Frank X Walker

The Negro Killer loosened me from my mortared kin. He was an urgent lover begging to be fed. Holding me about my middle, he swooped me up in an arc. He made me dance. Pausing me in mid-air before dipping and plunging swiftly, swirling me about in a worrying grey mist of madness. His aching fingers held me hostage as his silent slayer.

She lay in a satiated sleep. Teeth framed with red lips to greet me. Bessie, his bottom choice, bangs sliced across her forehead—my force awakened a sodden mass. Her blood discolored my red.

Front Page News

"HUNT BLACK IN GIRL'S DEATH"
a bold headline without mention of whether it be
black woman, black dog, black cat, black rat.
What IS known IS the GIRL murdered is white
'cause black girls don't make front page news,
five thousand police, vigilante squads, guns loaded
ordered to shoot any black whatever on sight.
Bessie lost, dumped, trying to save herself
digging, scraping her nails into the sides of an air shaft.
"NEGRO RAPIST FAINTS AT INQUEST"
First responders hear a lone woman's hysterical wail;
her screams subside. The paramedics feel her fading
pulse, dismiss her smashed skull, matted hair, blood
glued. Uneven tan bodies become one tenor sax moanin'
missing brown female bodies as revival hymn.
Someone they thought they knew—a woman easily forgotten.
Who is it? What broken, discarded blueberry, black body did they
    find?
On a lone note, Bessie Mears leaves her name scratched in concrete.

Fire is burning down below
If you ain't right, down you go
To original hot brimstone
Let you start right into moan
—Bessie Smith, "Moan, You Moaners"

Dancing Shadows

There is a dance they do. These two women,
whose disparate history makes them foe.
They are sisters of shade and sun.
Twin spirits, lost in Bigger's dream.

Bessie's skin kisses dusk. Her scars masquerade
in dark. Miscarried justice is Mary's lark.
Bessie knows too many Marys with false pleas.
Bessie remembers bitter births. Black boys
hung. Branches bend at weight tied by hate.

It seems unfair to disturb the beauty of trees.

Who are these two?
Dancing shadows who never meet.
Mistress and maid both laying dead.
One colored cream, the other caramel.

For the Marys

Can't no white woman talk about lovin'
my man more than me

Her lips ain't big enough to kiss pain
her America burnt in his skin

Can't no white woman talk about lovin'
my man more than me

'til she cut one from a tree or birth
one blacker than me

Still
She bet' not never tell that lie to me

Just bend your head way down and pray
to have the devil chased away
come let your souls be saved today
Moan. You moaners
—Bessie Smith, "Moan, You Moaners"

Bigger's Plea to Bessie Mears

Bessie forgive me for battering your flesh.
My crimson stain tatted your skin.
That brick was not meant as treasonous sin.
Cutting Mary's head made worlds mesh.
I burned her for your cries that did not win.
I killed you to cut my noose from all kin.
I beg you rewrite my story make it fresh.

Your wail frozen mid-note not cushioned by blues moan.
I abandoned you to a choir of maggot-faced men.
Tongues joined to lick at the naked dead.
Sharp nails scrape my cement cell wake my weary groan.
My muzzled manhood confined in this pen.
Howling loins haunted, hearing blues echo in my head.

I've lived a life, but nothin' I've gained
Each day I'm full of sorrow and pain
No one seems to care enough for poor me,
To give me a word of sympathy
Oh, me! Oh, me! Wonder what will become of poor me?
—Bessie Smith, *Wasted Life Blues*

Bessie's (almost) Rescue

"We remember you Bessie! Bigger ain't have ta do you like dat!"
Faded flower print dresses huddle, crowd streets, women, sucking
teeth, shaking heads.

Mouths unstuffed, spitting out sacred
black male parts. Speaking Bessie back into being—
defying learned allegiance to Bigger.

Was no posse to look for Bessie's body
frozen in slumped discomfort. No hands softening death's slumber;
her cry for help hardened by rage. She releases a soundless bawl.

Backward black men gather her loose skin
cover naked balls.

She is found; her mouth parted   unmet desires.
A certain good, a certain truth runs through black women
reading the Coroner's Report: Bessie beaten with a brick,
left to die in a black, iron, cold chute.

Bessie ain't do nothin' wrong in this life 'cept be black and woman.
If black ain't bad enough, bein' woman lessens their score.
The heavenly throng who hope for a cup of love like a bum hopes

for a cup of hash know Bessie ain't die from the cold or else they all be
    dead.
She ain't die from that brick 'cause that's what be beatin' them.
Eyes shut on trapped, sinking skin.

Did you ever fall in love with a man that was no good?
Did you ever fall in love with a man that was no good?
No matter what you did for him, he never understood.
—Bessie Smith, "Dirty No-Gooder's Blues"

Hereafter

I don' know why I never tol Bigger *No*.
Why I let him push me aside
then come back beggin' for mo'.
I don' know why I press my naps
fo' his sweat to curl some mo'.
I don't.   I really don' know why my woman
parts throb pleading his feel.
I knew I was what he needed when his tobacco-rubbed lips
trembled an after-cry.
I knew my brown skin was not a blinding white glare.
I was him in drag. A muddied mess. A clumped rag doll
wobbly-legged unable to set upright.
I don' know why a woman want to be the flat end
of his bed slipper—not needed in the hereafter.

Bessie's Drink

2 ½ jiggers blue bitters

2 jiggers spiced gumption

1 ½ jiggers raspberry rage

1 jigger salted tears

1 jigger gingered sass

½ oz. honey

How to Mix:

Glass: Highball or Martini

Whisky or Gin, combine all the ingredients.

Shake vigorously.

Strain into a well-chilled glass.

Garnish with lime-flavored grit.

Bessie Who?

for Sonia and Monifa

I was unseen like you
The one they call Bitch
The one erased like me

My dear sister, when they said all you need
is some dick, we all became nameless vapor.

My silence helped slay you.
My wilted voice helped
crown their fabulous cocks.

My dear sister, We become one
tongue to take back our names.

Baffled, I stood silent. I let them defame women.
Women who give birth groans, blues moans,
Nzinga war cries and Sojourner screams

waiting to throw their words back at them in a poem.

Bench Bop

I wanted to shove their giggles
down their throats. I wanted
to gouge out mean stares
while she lay, unmoved, belly up
soaking in September's sun.
Her untold story in loose things.

Nobody knows you when you down and out
I mean when you down and out

Her name hidden in a Cézanne
portrait: dark colors, an enhanced
somber green. She is real like
Ms. Rosie, Aunt Rubell, like Bigger's
Bessie, a forgotten half-note, a life
skimmed over. A matted-haired
woman with a white-knuckled grip,
bags close.

Nobody knows you when you down and out
I mean when you down and out

She, once ballerina, Wall Street
number runner, scientist, mother,

babbling woman raped of love.
Suffocating see-through plastic bags
keep her warm, smother nightmares, cradle
slumber, barricade white-fanged laughter.

Without a doubt, no man can use you
when you down and out.

His voice sounds like chimes, I mean the organ kind
His voice sounds like chimes, I mean the organ kind
And ev'rytime he speaks his music ease my troubling mind.
—Bessie Smith, "Any Woman's Blues"

Baaaaybe

I swear don't nobody say *Baby* like a black man:

Babe
Baby

Any rendition will do when he come creeping
in with the sun hitting his face while the moon's shining
on his ass. My eyes rolling so hard, I think they gonna pop
through their lids, arms akimbo, mouth wet with practice.

And he smiles—comes close up on me smelling like night's edge.
He almost whispers—a wicked whine to ensure my capture.
My hand smooths his wrinkled, empty space—
his side of the bed:

Hey baby.
How you doing baby?
I missed you babe.
Come here baby.
You know I love you baby.

Staring straight into his gravy-colored face, I tingle.
Thighs twitch enough to dampen all rage.

baby
babe
bae. I been trying to make it home to you all night
baby?
Don't act like dat baby.

There goes my knees collapsing me onto our bed. My head's in my
    hands.
Only half mad now.

He bends. His muffled   *baaaaybe*
vibrates my collar bone.

I'm wild about that thing, I'm wild about that thing,
Everybody knows it, I'm wild about that thing
Please don't hold it, baby, when I cry,
Give me every bit of it or else I'll die.
—Bessie Smith, "I'm Wild About That Thing"

Dick Dumb

\dik\ *n* \` dum\ *adj*

1: *n.* as reference to the male organ's inability to think and its ability
to incapacitate a woman's ability to make decisions
in her best interest once the organ makes contact.

2a: *v.* to eradicate the woman's sense to hear, see, smell, or taste
anything
that might alter her thinking for her own good.

2b: *v.* total penetration of a woman's spirit. *Slang:* dick-whooped
causing submission: ostracized from self.

2c: *v.* willing to forsake all womankind, ignoring any abuse to self.

3: *adj.* A term used to describe women who are silenced
and rendered invisible by their lust for the male organ.

They Said All She Need Is Some Dick

And if I get some dick, will I become dickmatized
able to scale tall buildings, leap from them
in a single bound to dodge dick daggers?
Will this dick heal my cuts from razors riding
my lover's tongue, slicing me wide when I fail
to glow from an orgasm I faked as mine?
Will it bless me? Will it anoint my forehead
forcing me to kiss the holy scepter before it enters
My Temple of Praise? And will I marvel at the dick's
trick to erect itself when I close My Temple's door?
Will this dick make me rich, shoot out gold dust
even though I have a diamond mine?
Will this dick ear fuck me, so I'm deaf, dumb and crazy
when I'm called *bitch, whore, scallywag, chicken-head*
or a man-hatin' madwoman if I talk about sisterhood
or survival?

Will this dick cradle me—the pieces of me chewed
on with crooked teeth that consider me exotic dark
meat, a medium-rare delight or honey-glazed treat
to make me whole—woman?

Clutching their panting cocks they don't say what kinda dick I need:
short, fat, stubby, long, pimply, pink, black, brown, beige, yellow

Any dick will do, like they all dicklicious.

All my life, I've seen pint-sized and full-grown men gripping
the front of their pants, jostling, fidgeting, repositioning,
making room for their maleness that is not privileged
in classrooms, board rooms, locker rooms, and at one time
white only bathrooms—only able to penetrate cell rooms
and me.

I've heard these same sad boys, these almost-men chant
this tired punchline like poets whose pens forgot to sing.

Bessie's Resurrection

after Nikki Giovanni

I am Venus, Hottentot, Yemaya, Olokun, Oshun. I am able to drown
all your lies and belch a new day. I swallow myself to become myself
sucking my wisdom like a mango seed. I piss lemonade, ginger ale,
sweet tea depending on what I desire. I see God when I come. My
orgasms awaken tribal orgies in Congo Square, Bessie's blues, Gospel
revivals. I am a repetitive riff—off-time. A shout without disclaimer; I
am mixed. Call me Magenta; all of me is Primary. I am polyrhythmic
consciousness, Black language of resistance. Splintering sound
haunting word whores. A reinvention of my own invention. Jesus'
voice claws my vocal chords. I don't whisper when I sing songs, when
funk rides my bones, when my spunk inspires me to fly, when I'm
ridin' my man to heaven and back hollering *hallelujah* just the same.
Blasphemy be damned! Sun's amber lips pucker, kiss well-traveled
feet. Somber moon caresses belly folds knowing all I hold. Stars wink
my destiny, spark against ebony skies praying in low hum. What is
that early whistle? What feathered thing sings her strange alarm? I
am red dawn trailing nights' lullaby. Many pieces of day uncounted,
abandoned, wisps of memory mistaken for unremarkable. A mystery
excavated, discovered and resurrected—
late.

SONG OF FLIGHT

She's wondering where her easy rider gone
. . . on a southbound rattler.
—Bessie Smith, "Yellow Dog Blues"

Rock Island Train

They came by way of Mississippi to Chicago
Windy City-blown dreams
I listen to their lax tongue
'Sippi sun soft, sliced
on Chi-Town's sharp tracks
plannin' to light up them city streets.
Singin' their blues between sidewalk cracks
between tobacco-tainted teeth.
Some settle into my red, green, creased
cowhide skin. Looking for lost pennies,
nickels, or dollars in case they want to go home again.
I embrace their battered bodies, sagging from the run.
Escaping outhouse stench, shotgun homes, lynch ropes.
Hearing echoes of names that sully souls.
Their sweat seeps between my leather worn by time
hands tracing their fortune in my wrinkled lines,
somethin' to tell them they going towards better,
before they step off to greet
chilly Chi-Town, without 'Sippi sun
blowing dreams in their faces.
Ducking icy blows, they stand sturdy.
Returning, only for sick kin.

Bessie to Bessie

She sang like what was crawling up inside me

was crawling up inside her too. She   heard the winds shrill against
rusty sundowns

a deep wailing of white clouds   long discordant notes howling
our blues.

Their lace swirling about my neck.   Letting loose whimsical
accomplices of sound

taking flight   high notes ripple through sky
landing

in Congo Square. Where we lip sync   liberation rites. Using our
bodies as drum

her voice as drum beating out loud   against an unrelenting earth.
Letting loose

ancestors who fly from shallow graves   echoes of field shouts riding
night's breeze

crooning between skeletal trees.   Something once alive begging
to be free.

Roaming blues searching for home   fighting dark spaces where
dreams climb

in a fog. An unnatural light resisting   gossamer hopes where ebony
sound reigns

above blue memories of song stamping place in unforgiving skin.

Passport to Freedom

1. Born 1896
2. Never married

Applicant: 5' 3 ½". High forehead, brown skin
brown eyes, sharp nose, medium mouth
round chin, brown hair.

3. Brother John told me: "you nigger women ain't never gonna fly!"
I made him stand as witness to all three lies.

Cockpit

Sun rises from the sea.
Rooftops are shimmering shards of light,
blood orange shades no one doubts.

There is a peace I feel
My wings dart between night and day

belonging to neither.

Juneteenth, 1925

Foot on wing, matching red leather cap and coat swing'n
mid-calf, I strike a pose. Sky is our Jubilee!

Dipping, swirling past clouds above a roaring crowd
I loop low. Like Harriet, I take as many that wanna go.

The plane my pencil, picking my speed, writing eights, I
claim sky. This ground don't own me. Up here, we all free.

Got the world in a jug, the stoppers in my hand.
Got the world in a jug, the stoppers in my hand.
I'ma hold it until you didn't come under my command.
—Bessie Smith, "Down Hearted Blues"

You Ask Why I Fly

I cloak myself in her billowy white ether.
Wholly woman in her expanse. She is not pure to me

Open. I dip my wings in praise.
She buoys my chase of her infinite beyond

ducking a jealous underworld. I am her tail
wind. Twin spirits circling a frustrated

sun overcome by a palace of clouds. You cannot

know her like me. I travel in and out gliding through her
many selves. A shapeshifter not defined

by dreams that do not fly.

Queen Bess

A shooting star singing through sky
An unfettered falcon without fear of flight
Flapping wings against a Texas one-room shack
Bessie couldn't jot down *her* Chicago-bound blues

An unfettered falcon without fear of flight
She came perched between clouds daring sons
Bessie couldn't jot down *her* Chicago-bound blues
She *be runnin' dem browns down*

She came perched between clouds daring sons
Swallowing men whole, spitting them out to fly
She be *runnin' dem browns down*
Swallowing her wind, she steals their laughter

Swallowing men whole, she spits them out to fly
She wants her men phoenix-like   lighting skies
Swallowing her wind, she steals their laughter
Hail Queen Bess! She claims her throne

She wants her men phoenix-like   lighting skies
She needs to walk before she flies
Hail Queen Bess! She claims her throne
Barren beds mourn her departure

She needs to walk before she flies
Twirling through rainbows
Barren beds mourn her departure
She teaches Nina to sing *Mississippi Goddam!*

Twirling through rainbows
Without Jim Crow, up there, everyone is free
She teaches Nina to sing *Mississippi Goddam!*
Prepares Odetta's crown, continuing freedom's fight

Without Jim Crow, up there, everyone is free
She is France's First Lady Liberty   chasing wind
She prepares Odetta's crown, continuing freedom's fight
She came singing about planes and being black and flying

She is France's First Lady Liberty   chasing wind
Her gut speaks about flying to feel alive
She came singing about planes and being black and flying
A shooting star singing through sky

Bessie Answers the Woman Question

Reporter: How do you think your flying will help the women of your
    race?

Crape myrtle trees, cushion in Momma's
lilac bushes. I birthed me. I gathered
myself from Waxahachie dust, white oil
sunbaked. I spoke myself into Being.
There's a school I'll build, a race who needs
wings to speed up things. I don't care what
they say about me.
The sky got me. It holds everything new.

Reporter: What about your fall?

Tell them all: as soon as I can walk, I'm going to fly!

The Truth about Flying

If ever the phone rang/ I'd fly home/ duty for a girl child/ repeated
    destination/
North or South/ lessons on flying/ instinct/ bird knocked from
    thatched nest/
I know my luck/ no cumbersome stoplights/ plotted speed bumps/
    grateful/ liked new home
smells/ countries/ cities/ far off/ Europe/ Paris/ Germany/ New York/
    Jacksonville/ Chicago/ searching/   free

I came home.

Paris Blues

His grey frayed scarf limply languishes
drunk with cologne.

Paris lights dim. I sniff its wool strands;
his scent lingers.

Unwashed musk masks time.
A threadbare thing.

Whiffs of him remain.

Brown skin's deceitful, but a yellow man is worse
I'm gonna get me a black man and play safety first.
—Bessie Smith, "Mama's Got the Blues"

Forget-Me-Nots

You don't get to wash away my smell
like I wasted yella on your skin.

You don't get to gargle with remorse
leaving your morning breath dumb.

You don't get to forget midnight's fragrance
nor our sweat-sweetened sheets.

You don't get to recoil your fingers after I
lay petal open to your guided flesh.

You don't get to forget my lullaby tongue
or my hips flying us to night's ledge.

You don't get to forget none of it when I
still hear my name riding us home.

Bessie's Men

Their want hisses, straightens naps cradling my neck.
I tingle. Lips moisten. Desire is not shy. It flits, flitters, flutters
flies above the Stroll's moonlit streets. Primitive rhythms fling
It into frenzy. They say they love me to make me stay.
Giggles tickle my throat at their believed trickery.
They do not know. I live free. Love's glow is not what makes
me shine or raise my wings. Boys are more trouble than men. Men
know. Money makes me nobody's but mine. Wife, Mistress, Queen,
names do not alter the course of what's living in me. Love's weight
does not ground my flight.

I have known men.

Flying African

And even though he said *you nigger women ain't never gonna fly*
I sprung free to test my wings.
And even though I thought I could stay snuggled in Jenny's pit, I wasn't
    scared
to spit sky.
And even though there were no attached strings, I was in awe
flipping wind, diving clouds.
And even though they came to witness my 351st solo flight, my
    performance
left them crying   wanting more.
And even though my bones lay mangled in crumbled dust,
their weight released   let me soar.
And even though they mourned my downed flight, they could not
    know
this lil' lemon gal was one of them Africans who could fly.

What about Bessie?

Black

grey black   Blue black,

black black   dusty black

Too black

for Bigger

Too black

for an America

that don't like him

that don't like

him and Bessie

Eye sore		Pushed back	Pushed out
Resisting	Pushing back	Pushed out	
Queen Bess	Flying	Pushing back	Pushed out
Aviator dreams	Resisting	Pushing back	Pushed out
Bessie Smith	Resisting	Pushed out	Pushed back
Back of lines	Back	Pushed down	Back out
Mississippi	Resisting	Pushing back	Death
on Route 61	Abandoned	On country roads	In chutes

clawing for air.

SONG OF FATE

Ever heard a sermon stir your soul?
Make you crave the River Jordan as you go?
Have you ever felt as though you'd like to shout?
Then come on and let them feelin's out, oh Lord!
—Bessie Smith, "On Revival Day"

Was Not Built to Break

Your heartache cracks your   voice
    steals your   breath
How to find home?
Not Dorothy's dreamland   the one you sang about
a place not visited since we were girls

our first recital/ twirled in pink-toed shoes
our mommy & daddy made us fashion-fair beautiful:
buffed us up
sprayed on Avon kindness to welcome a world
they prayed would treat us kindly.
We be *Purple Hibiscus* sure of our blossoming beauty
scenting up the world—
when too many others funked up our scent

And we forgot
We forgot
the old saints
the praying saints layin' hands on broke backs
singing saints with deep belly moans
troublin' the water with lavender & rosemary

Songs beating in their bellies   the old saints sang:

Hush, hush,
somebody's callin' my name
somebody's callin' my name
oh my Lord, oh my Lord
what shall I do, what shall I do?

And you rose from the water clean.

Native Daughter

Harsh gales rattle forgotten bones,
rattle walnut-colored woman's memory.
Back in '27, she heard Bessie singin'
loud enough to shiver storms:

Backwater blues done call me to pack my things and go
Backwater blues done call me to pack my things and go
'Cause my house fell down and I can't live there no more.

Now, she needs Bessie's sound to back the water down.
She wraps herself tight in a flag bent by storm.
Her teeth don't chatter. Her bones ache some.
Betsy's stars and bars keep her warm.

Blues Manifesto

Misty blues notes—diced
field hollers bounce off shack walls
promising justice

Bessie BE (A Praise Song)

after Monica Hand

Bessie BE

Savage		Beauty	You
	Abandoned		
Big-hipped		Bodacious	She
	Forgotten		
Black		Righteous	We
	Discarded		
Bessie		Be	I
	Abused		
African		American	Me
	Nameless		
Mule		Woman	Us
	Undressed		
Hidden		Bessie	She
	Erased		
Dark		Shadowed	We
			BE

Bessie's Woman

I drink her all
     Suck her flesh
Smell her through my pours

Giving thanks
I kiss blackberry lips
My taste does not make her shy

My jelly rolls
     are lush valleys
where fingers lose themselves

light shifts our cinnamon radiance
     Sprinkles night
on bodies battled in moonlight

dawn sings our blues

Pieces of a Dream

What happens when I wake out of arm's reach?
When your kisses no longer linger in my lips?
When I find out the song don't last long?
Are you going to leave me my soul?
Will Spring give dew-leavened petals,
or will I miss lilacs' bloom?
Will you rescue my heart from its frost
or eclipse smiling suns?
Will you offer Summer's breath?
Will church bells clatter
awaiting a holy redeemer?
Will they alarm the pad-foot thief
unafraid of the moon's brazen glare?
Will it dare conspire to resurrect
my soul or blink at its return?

S.B. on B.S.

She was my walnut wonder. My girl. Her hungry notes lasso'd
me. She growled them songs from the bowels of her belly.
Bessie was in my music. We was a harmony. I'd blow a beat
behind carrying the harmony home to either her bed or mine.

I was inside her but not like the music was. We made some
good sounds together. When she sang acapella, I could blow
her blues—make her notes purr around my melody. But a
muck was clogging her shoes, making her mean.

She wanted to feel safe in herself. She wanted the music clean.
Her nightmares haunted every note sang. She groaned our blues.
She knew their story. Every man that got gone. Every hunger pang.
Every hurt felt, she wrapped in song wanting to right wrongs.

Yeah Bessie was my girl alright. Her blues blossomed from a cotton
boll. Her croon crept up my skin pricked it good, till I saw red.
My clarinet wept and curled under her every note—wanting to ride
'top her broke chord or just sit inside daring her mean to break free.

Aggravatin' Papa, don't you try to two-time me
Just treat me pretty, be sweet!
I got a darn forty-four that don't repeat.
—Bessie Smith, "Aggravatin' Papa"

Hand-Me-Down Mean

Probably ain't nuthin worse than a hand-me-down mean.
A mean you can't even say is wholly yours. A tattered,
torn-at-the-seam mean; a you-don't-know-who-owned mean.

A feed-my-belly mean to keep from crushin' me.
It was my momma's and my momma's momma's mean.
A mean to fight. A mean to whip 'em good if NO was no good.

A two-sizes-too-big mean. A mean I had grown up in before
I had a chance to wean. My daddy's mean. My man's mean
dat got no safe place to go 'cept up in me. A stay-alive mean.

"Bessie mean," folks say. They only know a second-hand mean.
My blues is mean. Folk like Bessie's blues. The truth is mean.
You gotta be mean to tell the truth and drink the truth most days.

I wish I knew who this overcooked, leftover mean belong to?
I wish I knew how much mean I had up in me.
I wish I knew how to bring 'em out one by one.

I need a little sugar in my bowl
I need a little sugar in my bowl
I need a little hotdog between my roll
—Bessie Smith, "Need a Little Sugar in My Bowl"

Bessie's Every Woman's Blues

Bessie be every woman to me
   Singing her blues
   Singing her blues
She gulps the air he breathes
Oh how he makes her tingle!
Oh how he makes her wiggle with every squeeze!
She lives on moonshine-wrapped rainbows
sunk low in cotton candy pillows
leaning on weeping willow trees
   She cries: Hold My Mule!
   Hold My Mule!
That guitar singing her tune, kicking legs high
Her red heels fly soon
   She loves a good croon
Blessing her scars, she folds her hands in prayer
   O lord hab mercy!
   O lord hab mercy!
   O lord hab mercy on me!

I'm as good as any woman in your town
I ain't no high yeller I'm a deep killer brown
—Bessie Smith, "Young Girl Blues"

A Golden Shovel: They Call Me Empress

I hustle night. Showing you a tenth of what I'm
gonna do. Low humming half notes as
they skip between time—I'm a good
ole gal field hollerin' from Tennessee as
I strut stages. Feathers trailing with any
or no accompany. I am my own woman
sound. Making drunks sober, making saints shout in
tongues: " 'tain't nobody's business if I do." Your
uplift cry, drowned in crowds when I come to town.
Like Jesus nailed to a cross by his folks, I
Resurrec' from down home soot. Ain't
aimin' to please nobody scared of my tunes with no
polite howdy dos. My arms ain't long enough to reach high
for a praise you deny as mine. Your crooked yeller
mouths   twist   when you hear I'm
named Empress. You. Watchers of our race, stay a-
wake to chase my demon songs, those deep
belly moans you think otherworldly. My killer
notes, slice blue-veined native sons dressed in brown.

Glory glory,
Hymns are purifyin',
Glory glory,
Wash my sins away!
Lawdy lawdy,
Heal just like a lion,
Lawdy lawdy,
I'm reborn today!
—Bessie Smith, "On Revival Day"

Bessie's Last Song

I'm racing against a sun about to wink
racing against a rooster's holler
I want the moon to jump its own shadow
I plead for a stay of grace

I want to wane with an orange ray
stinging my day licked skin
Still got work I gotta get done
Still got songs I gotta get sung

I'm racing against a sun about to wink
racing against a field hand's holler
a moon about to jump its own shadow
pleading for a stay of grace on Rt. 61

Bessie's Final Moan

She could have been saved
Slipping away, she moaned low
Didn't bellow a tune

Singing "Hallelujah,"
"Blood ub da lamb"
Let your voices rise
Hear me talkin' to ya
Ain't got no time to sham

If you wanna to get to paradise
Repent without a doubt
Let the good lord hear you shout
Religion turns you inside out
—Bessie Smith, "Moan, You Moaners"

Why Bessie?

Church! I wanna ask you, "Why not Bessie?"

Ah when you ask the Lord "Why me?" He says, "Why not you?"

Does anyone know what I'm talkin' bout?

Bessie was like any of you. She was black. She was female. She was poor. She was in love. She was a daughter. She was a hard worker just like any of you.

"Why Bessie?" "Why not Bessie?"

Her name conjures up sleeping souls rocked in the belly of slave ships. Her blues first explode there in the bowels of this hellish ship that docked her and our forefathers on this foreign shore.

She came—womb weary having dumped her load in Yemaya's arms. She expels more seeds in planted rows after drinking Pennyroyal tea. This was her open revolt. She refused to birth anyone that wasn't free.

Her name is synonymous with both beast and wo-man. Teeth checked. Nipples pinched. Private parts probed in public places by pale-faced peeping toms.

She is a muddied map of southern red clay stuck to her heels, plowing through stubborn earth, pulling weight that is never hers to turn over soil to steal a yam to cook to remind her of home—where festivals welcomed the yams' arrival.

Church! I say, Church!

Ah know Bessie Mears ain't the first Bessie you knowd?! Who don't know an Aunt Bessie, Cousin Bess, Grandma Bessie, Momma Bessie, Queen Bessie or that woman called Empress that y'all sneak to the juke joint to see? Even Mr. got a mule named Bessie!

Her name is a collective song moaned into meaning. It means she knows something about somebody trying to ride the "Will" outta you.

It means her gnarled knuckles will not allow rings of deceit to slide over them for an unkempt promise.

It means her unlettered words from her fire breath speak her bruised beauty out of boxed lives. Bessie is the celestial charmer—the secret keeper of the soil's healing power. Bessie's name hums meaning into lives which are real and imagined and hard.

Her name like her life was a subtle blues note—a slow moan heard while spooning stew.

And Church! I say Church!

On that day when we thought she died. When they pulled her body out that cold chute, it was more than her that was raised from that place.

No! Brothers and Sisters, Bessie didn't die in that chute.

When she came up, all those Bessies who wear iron harnesses around their shoulders and on their backs dragging unwanted weight rose up too.

Yesssss!

All those Bessies who waited upon the Lord had their strength renewed and mounted up with wings as eagles; they ran and were not weary no more.

All those Bessies whose mouths were silenced with leather bits came out with her that day.

They escaped Shadrach, Abednego, and Meshach's fiery furnace of woe.

She was Jesus who suffered the blunt trauma to his skin but not his spirit to rise again asking, "Do you remember me?"

Church! Do you remember him? The one that died on Calvary, nailed to a wooden cross.

You ask, "Why?! Why Him?! This mighty lamb of the world."

Why?!

Why Bessie?

A woman who looked just like you blending all our knighted memories of kingdoms and Queens buried in the dust tracks of our tears.

I'ma close now.

But before I leave here today, I want you all to chew on this in the front of your minds. They say Jesus had 12 disciples but that ain't true. They forgot Mary Magdalene, and Jesus's own momma. So why Bessie? 'Cause Bessie was one of them too.

NOTES

Many of the blues lyrics that appear in this collection are cited by Melanie E. Bratcher in *Words and Songs of Bessie Smith, Billie Holiday, and Nina Simone: Sound Motion, Blues Spirit, and African Memory* (New York: Routledge, 2007).

I am indebted to the classic critical essay "Bessie's Blues," by Edward A. Watson in *New Letters* 38 (1971), 64–70, for the insight that the voice of Bessie Mears bears traces of blue singers of the period, including Bessie Smith and Ma Rainey.

In "Bessie's Gospel," the italicized words are from the song, "Moan, You Mourners" (often cited as "Moan, You Moaners"), lyrics and music by Spencer Williams, originally recorded by Bessie Smith on June 9, 1930.

The second stanza of "3 Bessie Bop" cites Richard Wright, *Native Son* (New York: Harper Collins, 2001), 215. The other italicized words are spoken in the novel by Bessie Mears.

The headlines in "Front Page News" are also drawn from *Native Son*.

In "Bench Bop," the italicized words are quoted (or in some cases adapted) from the song, "Nobody Knows You When You're Down and Out," lyrics and music by Jimmy Cox, originally recorded by Bessie Smith on May 15, 1929.

The epigraphs preceding "Rock Island Train," "Queen Bess," and "Flying African" are drawn from Doris Rich, *Queen Bess: Daredevil Aviator* (Smithsonian Institution Press, 1993).

The title of the poem "Was Not Built to Break" is drawn from Whitney Houston's song "I Didn't Know My Own Strength" (*I Look to You*, 2009).

The epigraph to "S.B. on B.S." is drawn from Sidney Bechet, *Treat It Gentle: An Autobiography*, ed. Rudi Blesh (New York: Da Capo Press, 1978).

In "Bessie Answers the Woman Question," the last line of the poem is taken from an unpublished article written for *The Chicago Defender* in 1923.

ACKNOWLEDGMENTS

Richard Wright's character, Bessie Mears in *Native Son*, would still be one of the least discussed characters in literature if it were not for my sister-friend and mentor Monifa Love Asante, who asked me, "What about Bessie?" and if one of my favorite teachers, Sonia Sanchez, had not reminded me that my poems are my breath and my response to injustice. I thank Spalding University and my mentors Greg Pape and Maureen Morehead for providing me the breathing room to express my vision. I also thank my Spalding University family, who listened and encouraged me to explore the many sides of Bessie, especially Jerrod for that Bessie Smith CD, and my cheerleaders: Kiietti, Leah and Candace. Finally, I thank the Callaloo Poetry Workshop Fellows and Greg Pardlo, for making me see what I was missing.

I am forever grateful to my parents, Carol and Julius Collins, who have always supported and encouraged me to write and to dream. "Damn, didn't Bessie have one good day?" is for my daughter, Kali, whose question reminded me of the complexity and layers of Black women's lives. I'm so glad she chose me to be her mother. Thanks to my cousin Lorraine for reminding me to tell a story. Many thanks to my crew of artist-editors to who believed in my work and wanted to assist in making it great: Tiffany Austin, Melanie Henderson, Antoinette Brim, Georgia Popoff, Tony Medina, Kenneth Riggins (for introducing me to Sidney Bechet's book), and my other artist friends who pushed me to be my best by being their best: Collette Williams, Monica Hand, Damaris Hill, Ra and Sweet and Natural for giving me the space to try new poems on new ears and a big hug to countless family and friends who continue to lift me up and keep me in prayer.

My deepest gratitude to Sam Grisham for the brilliant painting that graces the cover of this book, and my thanks to book editor Samantha Pious for her keen eye and patience.

Thank you to the editors who first published these poems, some of them in slightly different versions:

50/50: Poems and Translations by Womxn Over 50 (QuillsEdge Press, 2018), edited by Ann Davenport: "Hand-Me-Down Mean," "Paris Blues," "Bessie's Men"

Revise the Psalm: Work Celebrating the Writing of Gwendolyn Brooks (Curbside Splendor, 2017), edited by Quraysh Ali Lansana & Sandra Jackson-Opoku: "Washer Woman," "a burning lesson"

Women Artists 2017 Datebook (Syracuse Cultural Workers, 2016): "Washer Woman"

Black Gold: An Anthology of Black Poetry (Turner Mayfield Publishing, 2014), edited by Ja A. Jahannes: "They Said All She Need Is Some Dick," "UPSOUTH"

Some of these poems first appeared in the following journals:

Pittsburgh Poetry Review: "Bessie's Cry," "Bigger's Plea," "Bench Bop"

The Berkeley Poetry Review: "Why Bessie?"

Black Magnolia Literary Magazine: "Bigger's Plea to Bessie Mears," "Rock Island Train" (as "Meridian-Chicago Bound," "Native Daughter," "Queen Bess," "Elisheba"

ABOUT THE AUTHOR

Kimberly A. Collins gave voice to the movement against domestic violence with her poem, "Remember My Name," which has become a staple of Domestic Violence Awareness Month observances. Collins has facilitated writing-for-healing workshops for almost 30 years. Her inspirational weekly blog became the book *Choose You! Wednesday Wisdom to Wake Your Soul*. She attended Spelman College and holds a BA from Trinity University, an MFA in poetry from Spalding University, and an MA in American and African American literature from Howard University. Her poems have appeared in *Pittsburgh Poetry Review*, *Black Magnolias Literary Journal*, *Berkeley Poetry Review*, and other journals, as well as in the *Women Artists 2017 Datebook* (Syracuse Cultural Workers, 2016), and in the anthologies *Word Up: Black Poetry of the 80s From the Deep South* (Beans and Brown Rice, 1990), edited by Kalamu ya Salaam; *In the Tradition: An Anthology of Young Black Writers* (Writers & Readers, 1992), edited by Kevin Powell and Ras Baraka; *Theorizing Black Feminisms: The Visionary Pragmatism of Black Women* (Routledge, 1993), edited by Stanlie M. James and Abena P.A. Busia; *Fingernails Across the Chalkboard: Poetry and Prose on HIV/AIDS from the Black Diaspora* (Third World Press, 2007), edited by Randall Horton, M.L. Hunter, and Becky Thompson; *The Nubian Gallery: A Poetry Anthology* (Blacfax Publications, 2001), edited by Bob McNeil; *Black Gold: An Anthology of Black Poetry* (Turner Mayfield Publishing, 2014), edited by Ja A. Jahannes; *Revise the Psalm: Work Celebrating the Writing of Gwendolyn Brooks* (Curbside Splendor, 2017), edited by Quraysh Ali Lansana & Sandra Jackson-Opoku; and *50/50: Poems and Translations by Womxn Over 50* (QuillsEdge Press, 2018), edited by Ann Davenport. Collins is a Callaloo Fellow, and teaches English and creative writing at Morgan State University in Baltimore.

ABOUT INDOLENT BOOKS

Founded in 2015, Indolent Books is a nonprofit poetry press based in Brooklyn, with staff working remotely around the country. In our books and on our website, Indolent publishes work by poets and writers who are queer, trans, nonbinary (or gender nonconforming), intersex, women, people of color, people living with HIV, people with histories of addiction, abuse, and other traumatic experiences, and other poets and writers who are underrepresented or marginalized, or whose work has particular relevance to issues of racial, social, economic, and environmental justice. We also focus on poets over 50 without a first book. Indolent is committed to an inclusive workplace. Indolent Books is an imprint of Indolent Arts, a 501(c)(3) charity.